VICTORY

THE SPIRITUAL FOUNDATION FOR SUCCESS IN SPORTS

BY
MARK E. WARD

emerge
publishing

TULSA, OKLAHOMA

17 16 15   10 9 8 7 6 5 4 3 2 1

VICTORY — The Spiritual Foundation for Success in Sports

©2015 Mark E. Ward

TULSA, OKLAHOMA

Published by:
Emerge Publishing, LLC
9521B Riverside Parkway, Suite 243
Tulsa, Oklahoma 74137
Phone: 888.407.4447
www.EmergePublishing.com

Cover Design: Christian Ophus | Emerge Publishing, LLC

Library of Congress Cataloging-in-Publication Data

BISAC Category: REL012070 Christian Life;
                SPO041000 Sports Psychology

ISBN: 978-1-943127-07-8 Paperback
ISBN: 978-1-943127-08-5 Digital

Printed in the United States of America.

Acknowledgements

I want to thank the following people for their support and encouragement during this work:

My wife Carrie

My children:
Preslee, Luke, Parker, and Grace

Pastors:
Mark Haney
Ty Barker
Special thanks to Marilyn Price

My parents:
Bob and Sharrie Ward
Gregg Ward
Pam Heusman
Family and Friends

Also:
Travelers Baseball
Coaches Aid.com
Jason Swanson
Heath Ritchie

The booklet "Revelations of Infidel Scientists" by my Great Great Grandfather: Dr. Philip Stanley Hocker. Thank-you for your inspiration.

TABLE OF CONTENTS

Introduction

When you spend a lifetime wrapped in sports, you learn many things. As the author of this book, it is my goal to give back a portion of the lessons that sports have given us as it pertains to "Winning" and "Life."

Playing and coaching under some of the most successful coaches that youth and college sports can offer has led to a great deal of this writing. Of course, none of this can replace the twenty-five years spent in the team huddle and seeing the success and failure of young athletes with my own eyes.

I have concluded that sports give us something much greater than winning or losing. They often define who we are at any given point of time. Who we are refers to emotionally, mentally, physically, and spiritually. It has become clear to me that as people we are on a "JOURNEY." That journey is to grow to know the "truth" about who we are and what makes us fail or succeed! It also tells us about the choices we have as we follow this path to a destiny!

Team sports place us in a small group environment that resembles the world that we will face as adults. That "sport" environment tests us with success and failure, and the results of our choices will determine our future. During this journey, we must learn to make decisions that either help or hurt us when becoming players and adults.

I have concluded that people's interpretation of the things we learn from sports isn't sufficient when we realize what's at stake. Youth sports in America is the greatest single teaching tool available to prepare kids for life. That responsibility cannot be taken lightly!

After coaching dozens of championships and watching hundreds more with coachesaid.com, I have seen the tears of joy and pain! I have seen emotions tested and practically every reaction that championships create. It is clear to me that the responsibility that coaches and parents have will MOLD the foundation of the youth that are entrusted to us. If we determine that this responsibility truly is that GREAT, we MUST take the initiative to create a FOUNDATION and a PHILOSOPHY that match the importance of our position.

I have concluded that this foundation and philosophy require truth, making good choices, sacrifice, discipline, and love. The more I have implemented these principles and sought to become better at my job, it became EVIDENT that the TRUTH found in the WORD of God reflects the EXACT philosophy necessary to accomplish our goals.

As a player, parent or coach it is important that we realize what sports teaches us about life. We all have an opportunity to apply God's principles to our settings and situations, which will create everlasting character.

The principles of this foundation taught from the Word of God WORK every time!

In this writing, a foundation has been created to help players, coaches and parents. It addresses the five basics: truth, choices, sacrifice, discipline, and love. It also breaks down the role of the coach, parents, and players and how the communication of this core group is vital. Successful stories of testimonials, philosophies, and revelations are introduced to support the foundation of how God's Word works.

God's word and His plan for life has been diminished and I believe God has called all of us for a time such as this, to stand together to raise up this next generation. Sports are so important in today's society that we have a great opportunity to utilize its value to mold a generation that will reestablish the true foundation of God in Jesus Name! If you are a coach, parent or player the concepts in this book will help give you guidelines, it is simply a work to inspire you to follow God's plan in your own environment and make a difference.

Understand that we have a GREAT responsibility. Let's start applying a foundation that is guaranteed to work.

As a coach, I don't need the CREDIT. Young lives are in the balance. We need to put our pride in check and let the Creator of life teach our youth what they were created to learn. After all, He is GOD!

Mark Ward

Photo by CoachesAid Staff

CHAPTER 1
BACK TO BASICS

Applying the truth, which is found in the Word of God, to the team group dynamic and teaching players this perspective is the foundation for "success" in team sports.

Success in sports comes in multiple ways. It has become common in society that success is determined by wins/losses or championships. Those are visible and notable to the media and to the public. Therefore, they are viewed as being the ultimate scale for accomplishment.

"Back to Basics" defines the ways that youth sports are different than college and professional levels. The players at the next level have the potential and talent. That is why they were chosen to those teams by contracts and scholarships. The same media-driven philosophies and breakdown of professional athletes' character should not be completely transferred to youth programs, for it's not the same.

In high school sports, wins and losses should be viewed as an outcome or a result from the proper foundation. The foundation should be the first priority. Often, the wins and losses are not controllable by the team. Wins and championships are controlled by potential of the group. In this case, potential refers to "TALENT."

Professional sports can control the talent for which they pay. Therefore, the measure of success is directly proportionate to wins and losses. This is not true in high school sports. The amount of talent, or the lack thereof, is outside the control of the coach. Therefore, the success of high school sports should be based on how we utilize the team setting and implement a foundation to create character and values that will help prepare students for life while reaching their maximum success level based on the group potential.

Ninety-nine percent of players will not play professionally and 99 percent will not win a state championship. Although striving to be successful and to win are key elements that team sports are evolved around, these cannot be the "end all" of determining accomplishment.

"WINNING IS EVERYTHING" is a motto often used in America. It is misrepresented as the overall evaluation of success. An individual and team can do absolutely everything possible and still not win the game. This motto – WINNING IS EVERYTHING – really comes from coaches wanting players to strive to be the best they can be. Actually it is an uncontrollable and often unattainable "outcome" that keeps us hungry for perfection. We must evaluate success by the accomplishments that it took to create the best possible performance based on the group's potential.

The foundation discussed in this book is created to educate coaches, parents, and students about the reality and truth of youth sports and how all involved can reach their goals if they are defined properly. When the foundation is understood and implemented to the team accordingly, all involved can and will reach their potential.

Photo by CoachesAid Staff

CHAPTER 2

"THE CORE GROUP"
KNOWING THE POTENTIAL OF A TEAM

The "CORE GROUP" will be referred to throughout this book. It is made up of the coaches, parents, and players. This group ultimately should have the best interest of the players' future in mind and together should help create a foundation for success. The coach should publicly express the team's overall potential and define their goals together in a group meeting. The coach is the AUTHORITY and this must be understood, but open lines of communication must be created from the onset of a season. It is important that the coach, players, and parents hear the truth about their potential in a group setting. Often, it surprises parents to hear what the players think their potential is.

The group will get a better understanding of which players are viewed as the "best players." This type of group meeting to determine potential is a very enlightening way for all to place their priorities on COMMON GROUND!

The coach can hear all parties and speak his own opinion to the group so all involved can move forward with clarity of their goals. Jealousy and hidden agendas are often rendered harmless at this point.

Having better athletes does produce the most winning when it comes to being on the field, but it doesn't mean that they reach their potential any more than a sub 500 team. In fact, if the truth be known, the team that achieves the most rarely is the team that wins the trophy.

The message that society sends to teams today is that if they don't win the trophy, then they are failures. It also might tell them that they did their best while reminding them that their best wasn't good enough.

Success should be based on how far a team developed individually and corporately as a group over a time frame or a season. It should be rewarded as well based on the potential and the amount of growth achieved.

We must make our goals clear and understand that our prize should be based on reaching the maximum amount of performance that can be achieved based on the team's potential by the end of the season. Winning and losing and how we accept it should be based on the "truth" about who the team is as a group and as individuals.

The truth found in the Word of God is the perfect foundation from which life evolves, and it is likewise true with a team.

God made each of us to seek the truth in every situation. Coaching or playing sports is no different. Telling players and parents what "THEY" want to hear only makes a coach's job more difficult. The truth about who they are is what they want. They need a coach to be honest.

We need to explain to players and to the team who they really are as we evaluate their "potential." Also, we need to set their goals as high as we can to keep them hungry to achieve even more, knowing that we are setting out to be the best we can possibly be and passionately pursue this level. This is a level that can't be measured by winning or losing as its basis. A team can lose a game and far exceed its maximum potential in the loss. The best team doesn't always win a trophy!

Photo by CoachesAid Staff

CHAPTER 3
THE FIVE BASICS OF COACHING

Over a thirty-five-year period, I have been around the game of baseball for more than seventy games a year. Moving from a batboy, to player, to assistant coach, and ultimately the head coach has given me a unique perspective on the key ingredients that make up the best foundation.

It was obvious throughout my career that there are numerous variables that allow for team and individual success. Those variables I perceived to be too many and often too difficult to control from one single foundation. I found throughout my career that this perspective was not true. There was a foundation that would handle every situation we face.

I have seen just about every type of player, parent, and coaching style along with about every personality that goes with them.

After finding an intimate relationship with the Lord Jesus in March of 2000, I began to grow in the knowledge of the Word and the wisdom that the Holy Spirit has available to us. As sports and Jesus began to walk together in my life I gained a new perspective to the approach that would create the most solid foundation and eliminate the variables that seemed too overwhelming and often out of my control.

The question began to go off in my head that if God's Word is the absolute "truth" for us, then why isn't that same "Word" the foundation to teach in team sports? The answer revealed itself to me. The Word of God is the foundation for everything in life. God created everything and His Word is absolute. It is the foundation of life so therefore it has the power to make us successful in every situation that the "truth" of the Word is APPLIED!

Although God's Word is so big and His plan is far beyond our comprehension, we will start to create a foundation for success based upon the Word of God.

As I began to break down the years of experience of the game, I have formed a conclusion to this foundation. If we break our coaching philosophy down into five basic foundational teaching platforms, we can create a pattern for "SUCCESS" each and every time. I call them "The Five Basics of Coaching." They are truth, choices, sacrifice, discipline, and love.

These foundational teaching platforms, when taught from the Word of God, present a level of success on all aspects that lead to inevitable "victory." God's plan works in all things!

TRUTH

Players must know the truth about who they are individually and who they are in the team setting. The "truth" about a player must be obtained through evaluation. Therefore, they are consistently growing towards becoming a better player and person. It is the same growth that we go through as Christians. Coaches must be "HONEST" in their evaluations along the way and continually remind players of their accomplishments as they develop. As a result, TRUST WILL BE CREATED BETWEEN THE COACH AND PLAYER. A kind word and hard work with individuals will pay off.

Often players that start off slower in a sport or behind other players athletically move up and often move past previously more talented players over a period of time. Their foundation created with the truth will allow for the maximum amount of growth in character which leads to the most development in a given sport.

Identity is the key. A player will create a "TRUE" identity about the place they are at as a player. This perspective will allow them to reach the highest level of achievement based on the potential for growth created from the truth about where they are and where they intend to get to. This growth now becomes a realistic goal that can be established "by the truth."

Players are often given unrealistic goals and evaluations of where they are at from their parents and loved ones. That perspective almost always differs from the evaluation of the coach. Since we can conclude that the parent's perspective is not usually the "true" perspective, we must conclude that the coach's perspective most often is based on a more unbiased "truth." This coaching perspective is often not accepted or appreciated by the parents, and thus creates a conflict.

The following scripture from the Bible tells us about the "truth" as a foundation. John 8:31-32 says, *"Then Jesus said to those Jews who believed Him, 'If you abide in My word, you are My disciples indeed. And you shall know the truth, and the truth shall make you free.'"*

In these verses, Jesus tells us to abide in HIS Word; then we will be HIS disciples. Then we will know the truth, and the truth shall make us free. Therefore we must come to the conclusion that if this scripture passage is correct, then if we are not abiding in the Lord's Word, we do not know the truth. Therefore, we are in bondage and are not free!

It works the same in team sports. Often, a player's perception of the truth about his ability differs greatly from his or her parent's opinion or the coach's opinion. After studying the carnal nature of people and trying to determine their perspective of "truth," I have come to many conclusions and very few, if any, line up with what the Word of God tells us about the "truth" of God.

It is clear that the "world" is speaking a lot of things to people, and they are choosing to "accept" certain things as the "truth" and either good or bad for them. It's the same with young players on a team. They have a choice based on the knowledge they have gained to make decisions on basically every choice that they face. If a player's peers or even parents are unwilling to tell a player the truth about who they are athletically, it is the same as the false teaching that our youth are hearing from the world. Deception has a foothold.

How many different opinions and people are young players listening to who do not know the Word of God when making important decisions in their life? I started to be on guard of who was speaking into the life of my players and whether or not their plan came from a TRUE perspective that lined up with the Word of God!

I determined many things when I was seeking the Word of God to find out about the choice we have. First of all, the word "truth" is mentioned 237 times in 224 verses, all referring to the truth of God or the truth of HIS word. I have concluded that if truth of God's Word is the foundation, and of great importance for me to know, then there must be another "truth" or in this case an opinion that is masquerading as the truth that I need to avoid.

When we refer to the scripture listed previously, we must understand that something is keeping people bound that is either not the absolute truth, or perceived by people as something that is masquerading as the truth. If it doesn't come from God, then it is an opinion of the enemy. I believe the great majority of players are going through a season in sports in bondage from following a voice that is deceiving them. It often comes from peers or a parent.

Proverbs 12:26 says, *"The righteous should choose his friends carefully, for the way of the wicked leads them astray."*

A player must be given true direction and guidance as to how to improve his position on the team. It comes from a coach taking time with them and getting to know what motivates them and how they react to situations. The coach should understand the player's situation at home and the false teaching that they are receiving so they can know when the individual is being affected negatively by his environment.

THE TRUTH SHOULD NEVER BE DELIVERED FROM A COACH IN A WAY TO HARM! It must be delivered with "LOVE" and based on the coach's opinion that he gained through hard work and thorough evaluation.

Time and time again I have seen a player that simply

wanted his coach to speak the truth in love and also encourage them to work hard to grow in his skills and character to reach his or her full potential. Even if that potential is minimal, the player will feel accepted and will give everything "HE" has to the team and coach.

Settling for telling players and parents what "they" want to hear only creates more confusion and false self-esteem that is foundationally detrimental to the individual and the team!

CHOICES

Players must be taught to make good "choices." The question they need to ask is, "Are my priorities in order?" We need to know the importance of the decisions we make when it comes to training, working hard, attitude, and performing. Some choices affect the team and others affect the individual. When the choices for success are made clear to the individual and team, then it is up to the player to choose the direction that leads to improvement and ultimate success. It takes discipline to be able to make great choices consistently.

One of the biggest choices players must make is how to treat teammates. Keeping the same unselfish mind-set and helping others on the team is very important in creating unity, trust, and respect. Players will face difficult choices on and off the field. They can choose to react positively or negatively. Their choices will determine their future. If too many players react negatively in adversity, then the team's future is bleak. It is a mind-set that must be taken under authority by the coach. Negative attitudes cause internal self-destruction of the group and will cause the team to break under pressure.

There has to be a way to choose the right things when being a part of a team. We must turn to the foundation found in the Word to bring us understanding of how to choose.

A player's attitude toward the game and teammates is a choice. When a player has a big ego, he is setting himself up for failure under pressure. Humility and hard work are always the best choices when being a team leader. Players will naturally follow a teammate who makes great choices and shows respect to each player on the team, top to bottom.

Players on the team know when their leaders have the right attitude and approach. It does not matter how good a player is if he makes bad choices on and off the field. He will lack respect from his or her teammates. This type of player is destructive to the team and will cause team blowup under pressure situations.

The Word of God tells us in Matthew 5:38-44 NLT:

"You have heard the law that says the punishment must match the injury: 'An eye for an eye, and a tooth for a tooth.' But I say, do not resist an evil person! If someone slaps you on the right cheek, offer the other cheek also. If you are sued in court and your shirt is taken from you, give your coat, too. If a soldier demands that you carry his gear for a mile, carry it two miles. Give to those who ask, and don't turn away from those who want to borrow.

"You have heard the law that says, 'Love your neighbor' and hate your enemy. But I say, love your enemies! Pray for those who persecute you!"

Jesus is telling us that it is a "CHOICE" how we react to situations. Unfortunately, our emotions get in the way and we react differently than what the Word teaches us, especially in situations under pressure. Pressure always exposes our foundation. If we have built a solid and humble foundation that parallels what is in the Word, we have established a platform that will stand firm under even the most extreme pressure. Team and individual success depends upon a foundation that is established by making great choices.

SACRIFICE
SACRIFICE WINS CHAMPIONSHIPS

Sacrifices cannot be made properly until priorities are created. The coach and players must have clearly agreed upon priorities. Sacrifices must start from prioritizing. Example: God first, family second, team third.

When choosing to make sacrifices to get better, the player must prioritize his time accordingly. If priorities change and are not consistent, then the results will be compromised, especially under pressure situations. It is a part of knowing who you are as a player. Your identity and character are tested in battle. If you have a foundation of prioritizing your life, then you create identity. This type of identity does not easily give in to pressure or fear situations. Sacrifice builds character! And sacrifice pays off every time when priorities are in place.

Jesus Christ is our greatest example. He sacrificed Himself for us. Christ became the biggest winner of all time! It is by modeling His example that champions and heroes are made.

When a coach can create this mind-set of sacrifice with his players, all will become champions for all the right reasons. They will set a great example for the players and teams to follow.

I made the case that if truth, choices, sacrifice, discipline, and love are the foundation that the Bible gives us, then we should be using sports to teach the same things to young athletes. The results are the same!

Sacrifice is the most important part of the foundation. All ten of the results listed later in the chapter can be created in the team atmosphere when the proper sacrifices are made for success.

DISCIPLINE

It takes discipline to make good choices and sacrifices. Discipline can be applied to a player when they understand the truth about the Discipline. Players will not accept discipline if the wrong motives or intentions are present. They can tell the difference. Therefore, truth is at the heart of all discipline.

It takes a lot of discipline to make critical sacrifices that lead to success. Making a sacrifice is not easy. It especially is not easy when the sacrifice to improve must take place daily. Discipline and commitment could be one and the same. They both play a valuable role in individual and team success.

There are two types of discipline when coaching. It is the discipline the coach hands down and the self-discipline that comes from within the players. Most players are not born with self-discipline. They develop it as they grow in character.

The coach's forced discipline is good on some fronts and can create a certain level of success. There must be some imposed discipline from the coach for a team to succeed at any level. This discipline is mainly applied to the immaturity of players who have no, or very little, self-discipline to stay focused on their own. Even if players create a high level of self-discipline, they need the coach to be the authority and impose a certain level of control to the group to keep team continuity in place, as individual self-discipline differentiates among the individuals.

When the proper character is established in a player, they will begin to discipline themselves. This is what we call self-discipline and it is the ultimate goal for a player to reach. If a player has genuine self-discipline, you can bet that they have exceptional character qualities.

Individual self-discipline should be the goal of a coach. When the discipline comes from within individuals, they will carry the team to their destiny. Self-discipline is a journey and will be established and increase as individual character increases by the foundation of the Word. It is the "TRUTH" of the Word that creates character. That character, when matured inside an individual, creates discipline that will carry an individual to "THEIR" highest potential. The coach can basically provide fundamentals and teaching and sit back and watch HIS individuals flourish to their highest success level, which is our ultimate goal explained during the pre-season meeting.

LOVE

For any of the top four to be effective, players and coaches need to love what they are doing. If players are not found to have this type of love for the sport, then it will be hard to create sacrifice, discipline, and trust and make good choices. Passion for what you are doing is vital for success.

Love operates on many levels. There is love for the game, love for competition, love for teammates, and love of success. No matter how you define the different ways love can be created on a team, it is vital to understand how important it truly is in the overall success of the team.

Talented teams that usually fall short of their potential are most often affected by an environment that has become uncomfortable and loving what they are doing has disappeared. Unfortunately, this happens a lot in team sports. Too many things get in the way of love for it to exist as the corner post for success. These items include: anger, jealousy, greed, envy, and even hatred. These emotions will take place between parents and teammates and are often directed at the coach. When these emotions are allowed to operate or get out of control from the core group and the coach, the foundation crumbles and success is far from attainable.

The biggest reason for these emotions to drown out the love of the game is lack of communication. When things lie in the darkness and are allowed to manifest, a team is doomed.

James 3:16 says, *"For where envy and self-seeking exist, confusion and every evil thing are there."*

Since the Word of God is 100 percent true, then this verse is TRUE. Therefore, we must keep jealousy and self-seeking in check. This can be done when these emotions are brought to the light and exposed. Then the focus on all the LOVE aspects can be reinstated.

It is the responsibility of every part of the core group to protect LOVE in the team environment and expose the work of evil and confusion that lie hidden in the dark.

There is a sacrificial and group love that also appears as a result during championship situations. When a team has fought their heart out and applied the mixture of truth, discipline, sacrifice, and made good choices, an overwhelming LOVE comes over the group. The love is bound from the togetherness and bond that came from a group laying down their jealousy and envy for one another. This feeling is better than any trophy. Love is actually a result of itself in this circumstance. The community, parents, coaches, and players enjoy this love as achievement together through the proper foundation.

When love is present and operating throughout the team environment, success is inevitable. Wins, losses, and even trophies cannot stand against the love that can be formed. Everyone will enjoy success when love is present.

First Corinthians 13:4-8 tells us:

Love suffers long and is kind; love does not envy; love does not parade itself, is not puffed up; does not behave rudely, does not seek its own, is not provoked, thinks no evil; does not rejoice in iniquity, but rejoices in the truth; bears all things, believes all things, hopes all things, endures all things. Love never fails.

THE RESULTS

Common sense tells us that this type of success can be created even when a team does not win a championship or have a winning record. It is possible to operate in the "truth," make good choices, sacrifice within your priorities, have great discipline, love what you are doing, and still reach the goals that were created properly among the "CORE GROUP."

Having operated under the "five" basics as a coach, I have determined that there are common character qualities and results that are achieved in individuals. The ten most notable include: commitment, unity, trust, respect, individual self-worth, belonging, faith in one another, commonality of purpose, love, and winning!

These are the type of results that as "coaches" we must be seeking. The wins and trophies give us some incentive, but what we are teaching the individuals about life is the basis behind our approach. Players can only follow the leadership that is put in front of them. When that leadership has the wrong foundation, the opposite character qualities are instilled. Some examples of those qualities include: anger, bitterness, insecurity, resentment, doubt, fear, jealousy, envy, greed, pride, and quitting. Unfortunately, more players gain their foundation from this list than the previous one.

As coaches we need to recognize when our players are going through the results above and make sure clarity of purpose and the foundation of what our goals are have been properly explained. A player and parent meeting should be called to help determine the path of success before the darkness has allowed time to create false accusations among the "Core Group.

Chapter 4
The Core Group

The "Core Group" for success in high school sports is made up of the coaches, players, and parents. This group has common interests for the overall success and must have a common understanding of the approach and philosophy that are being incorporated for success. The COACH should call the group together and bring all controversial issues to the light so that the understanding of what will take place is not misunderstood or manipulated by false interpretation that often comes from the "world" or the enemy.

The following scriptures found in Ephesians, chapter 5, are the most crucial for the success and the functional dynamics of team sports, or life for that matter. We must bring negative issues to the light so that the "true" understanding from the "Core Group" can be balanced, creating the greatest opportunity to succeed.

The following "truth" found in the Word of God, applied to the team setting, guarantees an outcome of success.

Ephesians 5:6-15 says:

Let no one deceive you with empty words, for because of these things the wrath of God comes upon the sons of disobedience. Therefore do not be partakers with them. For you were once darkness, but now you are light in the Lord. Walk as children of light (for the fruit of the Spirit is in all goodness, righteousness, and TRUTH), finding out what is acceptable to the Lord. And have no fellowship with the unfruitful works of darkness, but rather expose them. For it is shameful even to speak of those things which are done by them in secret. But all things that are EXPOSED are made manifest by the light, for whatever makes manifest is light. Therefore He says: "Awake, you who sleep, arise from the dead, and Christ will give you light." See then that you walk circumspectly, not as fools but as wise.

Ephesians, chapter 5, is telling us that anything that is left in the dark can be manipulated by the enemy. Therefore, without open lines of communication, we will have multiple opinions of situations, often none of which are the "truth."

Having a preseason meeting and allowing the coach to address his philosophy to the group is vital. This open line of communication, bringing any possible issues to the light, is vital. Questions from players and parents should be addressed at this time so everyone knows the philosophy and what will be expected moving forward.

The coaches, players, and parents must gain an understanding of how to visualize their goals and how to pursue the best environment to help young athletes develop on and off the field, preparing them for the challenges they face now and in the future.

Photo by CoachesAid Staff

CHAPTER 5
THE COACH

Coaches are in authority over the team. They are hired by a higher authority to do their job. Parents and players must allow the coach to coach the team and speak into their lives positive principles and foundational tools for development of the athletes. Having a preseason meeting and allowing the coach to address his philosophy to the group is vital. Allowing discussion and questions to take place are also important. It creates an environment based on communication.

The coach should be understood as having knowledge about the game and an approach that is superior to the players and parents. The element of respect that stems from his position must be understood and trusted as the authority.

When this level of respect is established, it is vital for the coach to stress his inadequacy and how he is capable of making mistakes, but he also has been given authority and his mistakes must be accepted as end all of decisions for the group. He is the "General" of the team. It is not a democracy! His decisions should not be a topic for discussion or ridicule and must be understood as the law of the team, even if he, "the coach," fails. The "submission" to him as the ultimate authority allows the group to continue to search for the best solutions to reach their goals.

When the group understands that they all will make mistakes during the season, they again will reach a common ground of understanding the approach they are utilizing for success. They have a parallel direction instead of going against the grain.

The coach should provide examples about how he has seen players' failures create character changes and principles that will help their kids grow for future life situations.

The coach should stress to parents that failure can and often is the best scenario for their child to face. It is difficult because parents want to help them out of difficult situations. Players must be allowed to make decisions about their future with the group on their own. They need to reach down and face the truth about who they are as a player and strive to become better.

Parents and players MUST be "SUBMITTED" to the authority of the coach. This submission is imperative to the success of the group and should be considered the #1 foundational piece for success.

CHAPTER 6
THE PARENT

Parents must allow the coach to coach. The coach's responsibility is the group. Parents must also understand that others, and the team, are the most important part of team sports. This creates competition and allows individuals to reach a higher potential. The potential is not just physical, it is emotional, mental, physical, and often spiritual. If the foundational basics are in place, then trust should be given the coach to operate in the best manner to help develop all the athletes, even if tough lessons individually are necessary.

Upset parents and players often realize in later years that the coach was right about what he was teaching an individual. They often seek out a coach years later and tell them they helped their child even though at the time they didn't understand it. THIS UNDERSTANDING SHOULD BE MADE BEFOREHAND SO THAT THE TEACHING AND LEARNING CAN TAKE PLACE IN THE PROPER

ENVIRONMENT. Young players and parents normally do not know enough about the overall sports environment to have an opinion to speak into the team as a whole. They must stay under authority, let things happen, and allow the coach to do his job!

Parents need to find a way to communicate their frustrations with love and respect. It is a choice! In the book of Galatians, it talks about the fruit of the Spirit:

But the fruit of the Spirit is love, joy, peace, longsuffering, kindness, goodness, faithfulness, gentleness, self-control. Against such there is no law. And those who are Christ's have crucified the flesh with its passions and desires. If we live in the Spirit, let us also walk in the Spirit. Let us not become conceited, provoking one another, envying one another.

Galatians 5:22-26

Parents must create an environment for their son or daughter to tell them the "TRUTH" openly about their situations. Most of the time the player DOES NOT feel the same way as the parent about his or her situation, and since they cannot communicate openly, the player will find a way to ESCAPE the conflict, often resulting in quitting for the wrong reasons.

How often do we talk about the parents' feelings when it comes to their child's position on the team? The problem is the word "feelings.

How someone "feels" is most often a contradiction of the truth about a situation. Feelings are discussed in the works of the flesh found in Galatians.

Now the works of the flesh are evident, which are: adultery, fornication, uncleanness, lewdness, idolatry, sorcery, hatred, contentions, jealousies, outbursts of wrath, selfish ambitions, dissensions, heresies, envy, murders, drunkenness, revelries, and the like; of which I tell you beforehand, just as I also told you in time past, that those who practice such things will not inherit the kingdom of God.

Galatians 5:19-21

Feelings more often than not lie to parents about a coach's intentions. Coaches do not have an agenda to harm a player. They do not wake up with a plan to take situations out on kids. They have more to worry about than hurting the players on their team.

Many times you hear parents say, "He is just mad at my son! So he is punishing him." That may actually happen on an occasion, but more than likely that is the escape for the parent's emotions when his or her child is not the star or key player on the team. Those emotions are often displayed in the stands to other parents causing them to question the coach's motives. This "Rabbit Trail" of bad feelings is now running rampant through the "Group" and hidden from the light. Unfortunately, a high percentage of team failure is caused by this vary scenario, and more often than not, it had nothing to do with the player or the coach.

A parent's fleshly emotions can cause them to make poor, irrational decisions that will ultimately cause breakdown of the team.

The best team environment is created when a coach and his players can be allowed to face their battles without parent influence. There "IS" constructive communication between parents and the core group, but they must be kept in emotional perspective by the coach and players. Understanding that parents have emotions about their child and allowing "grace" to the parent with love will often break down the negative impact on the team's success.

A parent can LOVE his child so much that they just want them HAPPY. If the player is happy being on the bench, then the parent often will be happy as well. The problem is that the "heart" of the player is hidden from being openly communicated and the reaction from the parent to lash out is nothing more than DECEPTION.

Parents need to understand that a player's character NEEDS TO BE TESTED AND PUSHED TO DEVELOP A HIGHER LEVEL OF GROWTH. That testing is either warranted and accepted or rejected and ridiculed, which breaks down the foundation and the relationship among the group.

Photo by CoachesAid Staff

CHAPTER 7
THE PLAYER

Players are under authority and are in the environment to learn. They should have very little opinion. They are KIDS that are in SCHOOL. THEY ARE OUR FUTURE AS WELL! People, such as the coach, are hired to teach them. Players need to stop acting like they are smarter than the coach! This should also be illustrated in the foundation meeting before the season in front of the Core Group.

Players should be taught the importance of the coach by their parents. If the parent chooses to disrespect the coach, the player will do the same. This causes a complete break-down of the "Core Group," and it will cripple the group's ability to succeed.

The players are moldable. They must respect the coach's ability and choose to react to criticism from the coach with integrity and do their best to do the things necessary in the coach's mind to succeed. It must be viewed as "the coach is RIGHT with what he is telling the player about his or her play." More often than not, the breakdown comes before the true intentions of the group have been communicated to the player or parent. We must bring clear understanding to the Core Group in advance of the potential misunderstandings.

Many times a player or parent could be correct in their interpretation of their individual's ability, but for that player's ability to fit into the overall scheme of the "TEAM" coming first, there may be a difference of opinion. If the team is first, then the sum of the whole working together must outweigh the individual pieces. This is a BIG misconception to individual players and parents.

One example I use to illustrate comes from basketball. A center might be better at rebounding than the forwards getting to play and may be a better scorer than the other four starters. But if he is the second best center, than he cannot be on the floor at the same time under the team concept. More than one center on the floor makes the "TEAM" vulnerable to pressing defenses and situations that require other skills on the floor.

Parents will often take the individual "player's" ability out of context and make a case about why he should be playing more, even if the team cannot function at the highest level with the outcome. Therefore, the "Core Group" would not be holding true to the team concept as its highest priority.

Players should understand that the coach cares about them and their future. The players are there to learn. Learning in team sports is more than math or science. They are there to learn about life principles. They are there to create character qualities that will last a lifetime. TEAM SPORTS is the only example of group dynamics in the school system that allow the type of competitive interactions that can resemble life. THEREFORE, PREPARE THEM FOR IT UP FRONT WITH A PROPER FOUNDATION FOR SUCCESS!

Photo by CoachesAid Staff

CHAPTER 8
CONFIDENCE, PREPARATION, AND SUCCESS

It is important that we realize a balance that will produce ongoing success as a player. There are three key elements that contribute in an ongoing pattern. They are confidence, preparation, and success.

These three work hand in hand for improving performance, but without any of the three the pattern is broken. A player must have success to gain confidence in his or her ability. This creates a willingness to prepare. Likewise, if a player prepares, he will gain confidence. That confidence will lead to success.

When planning for the season, a coach must prepare his players individually and in the team concept. This preparation will create confidence! When a player reaches a level of confidence in himself and his or her team, then success follows.

It is important for a coach to put players in a situation to succeed. The quality of teams on the schedule allow for this success. A balance of good teams and weaker teams will challenge players to get better and prepare hard, while the success they can achieve over weaker teams will also keep them hungry for improvement.

It is important to schedule enough games that the team should win and create individual accomplishment. Not always is this possible if a weaker opponent is not available. Sometimes this happens and teams are unable to generate enough success to start the cycle discussed.

A perfect schedule usually involves a balance of the abilities of opponents. For example: In a forty-game schedule, it should be a goal to schedule ten games that are so-called easy wins, ten games that are potential losses, and twenty games of equally matched opponents. If you can create this scenario, you will have the perfect blend of competition to create a balance in confidence, preparation, and success.

A few early season wins followed up by a couple of very difficult challenges is ideal for growth in a team. Scheduling of the season is way undervalued and misunderstood as a key to creating a successful program. An argument could be made that "scheduling" is one of the most important jobs a coach has.

This is very similar to life in general. If we prepare from the correct foundation, we will gain confidence in who we are. That confidence will lead to success in life. This type of preparation comes from the "truth" found in the Word. When we exercise the truth in our lives, we will produce good fruit and become a blessing to others. Preparing on the field is no different than preparing our hearts and minds to become successful in life. The better the coach's fundamental plan for us, the better hitter or fielder we can become.

God is the ultimate Coach on life. He created it. His plan, found in the Word, will prepare us for the challenges we will face. We can meet them with confidence, knowing we are prepared and destined to succeed!

CHAPTER 9
FOLLOWING LEADERSHIP

Possibly the greatest responsibility we have as coaches is leading by example. Throughout a ten-year period of leading a team, I learned that the players' personalities and reactions to pressure situations changed dramatically. The fundamentals of how to play and the practice plans remained the same. There was certainly an increase over the years in character, personality, steadiness, stability, and success of the players and the team.

In trying to identify the change, I realized it patterned a change that I had made personally. It was the change in priority that made the "breakthrough" difference in our success on and off the field. The priority of placing God first, family second, and sports in its correct slot in the order made everything come together. A lot of people talk about having this order of priorities, but very few truly operate in it. Matthew 6:33 says, "But seek first the kingdom of God and

His righteousness, and all these things shall be added to you."

Success in sports remained very significant in our approach. In fact, the passion and desire to do the best never changed. The results of following the "truth" about who we were as a team became our victory.

As I grew in the Lord, I found peace in the person I had become. God had a plan for me, and I began to realize that He had a plan for each individual player that I coached as well. This responsibility should never be taken lightly.

Early on in my coaching career, I believed success was attributed to emotions. If we could raise our level of anger, excitement, or energy high enough, it would bring us victory. The problem was that it was often misdirected and highly disrespected. This foundation was not built with any stability or cornerstone.

I found that controlling these very emotions allowed us to operate under a greater level of discipline and security in our ability to perform. The very emotions that one time caused our team to break under pressure eventually became the same emotions that broke our opponents.

As coaches, it is important to realize that players will begin to act the same way YOU do! I noticed this personality with my team. In my early years of coaching, I was undisciplined, angry, and over emotional under pressure. My players were exactly the same for the most part. In fact, some of them were more mature than I was about a lot of situations. That so-called "foundation" would often work when things were easy and pressure was at a minimum.

Growing in the Lord helped me to realize that there is

ONE universal foundation in the world that has no break-ing point. This foundation was created by God and simply "works" in every situation in life, because it's the "truth." Pressure has no meaning to the absolute completeness of God's truth through Jesus Christ. In fact, pressure is ren-dered harmless and meaningless when confronted with the proper foundation.

As I began to invest the "truth of the Word" into my play-ers individually and as a group, things began to change. First off, they saw me as a person who was leading them with a foundation that mattered to them. That foundation provided strength, stability, security, discipline, and trust. It actually had nothing to do with me; it was God's foundation that was being taught.

God created us to seek Him. Players wanted to find the substance of this "truth" that was inspiring them to succeed. No person in the flesh has this kind of stability. Only the foundation from the Word of God can provide it.

The subtle approach of investing in the Lord's plan to the team would grow throughout the season. Players would hunger to hear more and to apply it to their game. They had a passion to be disciplined in the areas where they struggled.

Revelation of applying scripture to our situations will come when we realize that players are often fearful about certain things. Looking up what God has to say about fear gave me an answer. Second Timothy 1:7 says, "For God has not given us a spirit of fear, but of power and of love and of a sound mind."

Applying this scripture over my players regularly worked. At first they viewed it as just something to say to make them feel better. Then the root would start to take hold in their hearts. It would "supernaturally" work its way into their foundation.

Sports cause individuals and teams to struggle and fail. It will be hard, at first, to explain to them that their failure would often be the key to their success. We must "fail" so we can learn from it and we can become better. Applying the scripture found in Romans 8:28 works in our personal life, and it will also work for individuals and a team: *"And we know that all things work together for good to those who love God, to those who are the called according to His purpose." Romans 8:28*

In coaching, it is hard to keep your foundation in place without outside interference. This interference can come from peer pressure, people in the community, and especially parents. They are unaware that they are harming the team's chances of success by criticizing or speaking about the team without proper knowledge. It is very important to keep the "TEAM" focused on your goals and foundation.

To keep our team perspective together, I often spoke Romans 8:31 over my team during our prayer time: *"What then shall we say to these things? If God is for us, who can be against us?"*

Being calm under pressure will start to come natural. It can take years of seeing pressure and applying the best plan under those circumstances to allow coaches to operate at a higher level when faced with it.

Sometimes players act cool when things are going well. They will play the game like "THEY" have everything under control. This changes when pressure hits, and coaches must learn to know the difference. A coach should know his players well enough to recognize it on their faces. When players are unable to handle the situation emotionally, you will start to recognize them holding on to the foundation they have been taught from the "Word." They will turn to the steadiness and stability that the truth gives them about their situation.

Nothing can replace a great foundation and experience seeing it work. The responsibility of leadership we have cannot be taken lightly. We are helping shape the lives of a future father and husband. Sports place us in an environment to create leadership. The leadership that our players gain can determine their future. To help create leaders, we must be a good leader first. Coaches should trust "God's" plan to fulfill the responsibility to their players. When we realize what's at stake, we come into agreement that they deserve the "BEST" we can give them.

CHAPTER 10
ESTABLISHING THE WORKLOAD

The workload responsibility of a coaching job cannot be taken lightly. We must bury ourselves in the responsibility and strive hard enough to set an example that can be followed. If we coach with passive emotions and half effort, we will receive the same from our players.

Youth players oftentimes are in a position to place their sport as the third priority. That means it is NUMBER 1 after the LORD and FAMILY. As a coach, we must recognize this and send the message that it has the type of value to us just as it does to the players. It goes back to prioritizing. If we place multiple things between our family and the team, we send a message that our focus is devaluing the players' efforts.

We must always stress God first and family second, but we must set a pattern through our workload that shows our effort is at least equal to or greater than the players' interpretation. Therefore, as coaches, WE set the BAR for workload!

Players will work just as hard as the example you put into your coaching. It follows the same example of life that says: "You get out of life exactly what you put into it, nothing more and nothing less." Effort can often speak louder than teaching. There is something about effort that makes players respond. It must be at the highest level of our approach. If you outwork your players on the field, they will begin to follow that same example.

It should be an endless pursuit toward the goal. If players realize how much their success means to you by your actions, they will respond with relentless effort when preparing.

CHAPTER 11
THE PAST IS THE PAST

It is important that the Core Group have a short memory of things that have already taken place. Good or bad, we must direct our efforts to what is next instead of what has happened. Our response to situations truly determines our future.

Staying away from the emotional highs and lows or our previous play will keep us stable and capable of making the next play at the highest level.

When bad plays are made on the field, it is important to move forward to the next play. It takes discipline to look to the next play regardless of how the plays before made us "feel." Good or bad, we must avoid the emotional roller coaster to create consistency. This foundation comes from knowing exactly who you are as a player and knowing that your preparation and best effort are "available" on the next play. It is about knowing the "TRUTH."

Our emotions or flesh will try to tell us either bad or good things about ourselves based on the previous play. It can lead us to doubt ourselves if we have made a previous mistake. That doubt begins to tell us that we can't do it. It lies to us about our ability and preparation. That doubt is a "LIE." It should not have the right to cause another mistake. Sure, we are capable of making a mistake on the next play, but it will not be because we expect it or invite it into our thoughts by telling us untruths about ourselves.

Good plays are "almost" always good for our future success unless we become elevated to a place of arrogance or pride to the point of inflating our ego, resulting in unstable thoughts. When we keep our emotions in check and realize that we are becoming better at our play and use the good things we achieve as motivation to continue to work to get better, we can build a strong foundation. When we allow pride to come into our thought patterns and lose our work and preparation habits, we set ourselves up for an emotional fall. We need to keep that good play in the forefront of our thoughts, but also keep in the back of our mind the discipline to understand that we must not elevate our pride to a place of breakdown. It is about balancing our emotions.

Players must understand who they are as a player. It is no different than life. When we are grounded with a solid foundation, we begin to create a solid "identity." When people become foundationally equipped from the Word of God, they start to cling to the identity that Christ and the "Word" have given them. That identity is unshakable.

When a player has the foundation found in the "Word" and knows who he is as a person, along with great physical fundamental teaching, he has the highest probability to achieve his or her maximum potential. When either foundation is lacking, they are limited on how much they can achieve. It basically sets parameters for our success on and off the field.

The Word of God teaches us that we need to be forgiven of our past mistakes to move forward with a clean foundation in Christ. This same concept is "true" in all aspects of life. When a player makes mistakes, either physically or mentally, they must move forward with the mind-set to simply be better. The player's response to mistakes will determine their future. Unfortunately, coaches and parents often reinforce the negative and break down the mistake to a level that can damage the player's identity. We must "teach" constructively and bring understanding regarding the mistakes, then encourage them to move on to being better next time under the same circumstances. It is not to ignore the mistake, but to address it as much as necessary, and then be finished with it and remind the individuals that it is in the "PAST."

When the entire "Core Group" has this foundational understanding, then the player can reach their full potential.

Photo by CoachesAid Staff

CHAPTER 12
CHANGING COURSE

During each season, a coach will more than likely need to make a course change. By nature people begin to operate selfishly and lose focus of the team concept.

There are clearly two forces at work in people. One is the works of the flesh, and the other is the fruit of the Spirit.

Galatians 5:17-25 says:
For the flesh lusts against the Spirit, and the Spirit against the flesh; and these are contrary to one another, so that you do not do the things that you wish.

But if you are led by the Spirit, you are not under the law.

Now the works of the flesh are evident, which are: adultery, fornication, uncleanness, lewdness, idolatry, sorcery, hatred, contentions, jealousies, outbursts of wrath, selfish ambitions, dissensions, heresies, envy, murders, drunkenness, revelries, and the like; of which I tell you beforehand, just as I also told you in time past, that those who practice such things will not inherit the kingdom of God.

But the fruit of the Spirit is love, joy, peace, longsuffering, kindness, goodness, faithfulness, gentleness, self-control. Against such there is no law.

And those who are Christ's have crucified the flesh with its passions and desires.

If we live in the Spirit, let us also walk in the Spirit.

As coaches we must be responsible for keeping the group on the path to achieve our goals.

We must accept God's Word as the absolute "truth." If Galatians 5:17 is true, then as coaches and players we are fighting constantly the two directions placed before us.

The season can become long and stagnant. We will be tested with success and failure. The flesh is weak and each season players begin to become more selfish and jealous by nature, just to name a couple fleshly qualities.

When this happens, it is important that the "coach" expose the work of the enemy in the individuals and bring their selfishness and jealousies to the light.

When we do this, it becomes clear to the group that God's Word is true. We must set aside our desires and embrace the plan of success that has been foundationally laid out for us in the Word of God.

As coaches we will begin to feel this course change toward the works of the flesh. We must bring the group together at the proper time and expose this failure among players and bring it to the light found in the truth.

Calling players out in their jealous ambitions and setting the course from the fruit of the Spirit into effect over the situation at just the right time, will propel the team towards their goals with a destiny guaranteed to succeed.

We come to the realization that as individuals we will perish in our own fleshly desires. The works of the flesh will cripple and destroy us EVERY TIME. We must get everyone to admit that we fall into this position by nature and humbly accept God's path to complete our journey. It is how God intended it to be!

Photo by CoachesAid Staff

CHAPTER 13
BEING CALM UNDER PRESSURE

As coaches we soon learn that our players pick up our personality. Whether we agree with it or not, players are watching every move the coach makes. When he is intense, happy, sad, angry, or calm, this is the personality that we are delivering to the individuals on the team. If our personality is to fly off the handle in the face of pressure, our players will act and do the same.

As a coach seeking God as a foundation, we begin to be secure in our decisions. That security and following the Word allows us to react with the fruit of the Spirit, which is found in Galatians, chapter 5: love, joy, peace, longsuffering, kindness, goodness, faithfulness, gentleness, and self-control. Against such there is no law.

By nature we react from the flesh, but we can form a new identity when we "choose" to walk in the Spirit. That very choice begins to become our foundation, and our emotions will bow to the goodness that is stored up in His heart.

By experience we will learn to actually balance the pressure with a calm peace. It is the opposite reaction that creates balance. When teams are slow and lethargic or as we like to say, going through the motions of the game, we need to get excited. At times it is necessary to provoke our players into intensity.

Do not get intensity confused with anger or other emotions. The greatest concentration and intensity are found in calm confidence. It is something that we have to learn to balance in our players for them to achieve their highest level of performance, especially in pressure situations. It is something that has to be practiced. The more times we can place our players under pressure and show the example of being calm and confident, the more they begin to become successful in spite of it.

Photo by CoachesAid Staff

CHAPTER 14
THE COACHING BOX

When discussing the role of a coach, I feel it is necessary to bring examples and truths from testimonials about coaching. As a baseball coach, I have fought many battles in the third base coaching box. When you are unable to play yourself, you live and die with every pitch. Over the years of coaching, things change. Following the Lord and imparting the things of God to my team started to transform my thinking. I began to see the players' personal needs at a higher level than the outcome of their performance.

Over the next seven years, our summer team returned several three-year players. Our relationships were strong and I understood their needs away from the field and the battles they faced at home. Some of these players were qualified and loved by how good they were at a sport. This began to work on my spirit. Players who were good kids had their identity wrapped up in their performance. It was the only identity that they really had. That identity was placed upon them from home.

Households that had their priorities out of order had placed this pressure on these young men. Therefore, failure on the field had become complete failure for their identity. This led me to begin each season with the same statement for players: "If you are loved and your identity is wrapped up in your success as a baseball player, you need to find another place to play. You are a person first and a player second."

It was becoming common for this team to win and win big. We had won the championship in four consecutive tournaments this season. The value of on-the-field success began to shift to the needs of the player. I later concluded that those needs should have been first from the beginning.

The fourth game of the tournament we were down a run with players on second and third. One of my players whom I knew very well was at the plate. I remembered praying many times for our success from the coaching box. God does care about everything! For the first time, I faced a crossroads in my coaching career. This player had been struggling and needed something to go well. The problem was that the root of his challenge had come from home. It had spilled over to his play. I stopped myself for a moment and said, "Lord, I don't know that it is best for him to succeed. He is missing the foundation from home that he needs to succeed past this level of play. That foundation will not change by him getting a hit and us winning the game. It would simply increase the pressure for the next time."

For the first time, my prayer and philosophy changed. I said, "Lord, Your WILL be done for this young man." He failed in his turn at bat. The team later won the game, but this youngster broke and hit bottom. He had a heart-to-heart talk with himself and his family. The bondage that the enemy had created was broken. From this night forward, he was a different player. The priorities were realigned in his life and success fell in place.

This revelation I received began to manifest itself daily. I began to look at the root needs of players and changed the way I had viewed my job. I began to share the Word daily and pray for their needs even more than before. All of a sudden, we were in the business of changing lives and helping establish the future for these young men. That value for them as people became the focus. Our players began to grow spiritually and physically. The outcomes on and off the field were miraculous.

Our program was dominating in a way that I had never seen. Most people believe that it had a lot to do with money, talent, and coaching. Those were factors that helped with our success, but the truth is that players began to KNOW who they were. Their identity had value outside of the box or the field. The future results of these players at the college and professional levels were the same. For the first time I felt as if we had understood and taught the game completely. Success was foundational and prioritized.

College coaches began to recruit our players and tell me that they wanted them because of the type of kids they were FIRST. This revelation that I received had made a huge difference. God was just looking for a situation where He could affect the lives of these young men. Being submitted to God's plan and fulfilling His Word in your day-to-day activities will change everything every time.

After watching a lot of startup baseball programs and young coaches, there is concern about the approach. I pray for them to gain the real understanding of what we are doing as coaches. I see young coaches who have placed their pride first. That is the place where I was. It is easy to believe because you win a game or championship that you have done a great thing. It is a good accomplishment to be successful on the field, but it should never be prioritized above the value of the individual. We have won more than thirty championships over seven years and not one was more important than any one individual's well-being and foundation.

If we coach from the Word of God and prioritize accordingly, championships will follow.

Photo by CoachesAid Staff

CHAPTER 15
MAKE YOURSELF OF NO REPUTATION

Many times young coaches are prideful with their place in authority. When I first became a coach at the age of twenty-two, I was looking for identity. I believed our success was about me as the leader and I was at least partly deserving of the credit. There were ups and down as far as on the field success was concerned, but the foundation and the perspective of the teams were tainted. It was murky and cluttered.

In 2001 I became the head coach of the Oklahoma Travelers. We were in a situation to move the team to a new city and get a fresh start. The move was a good one on many fronts. I remembered praying about where to go with the team. I was building a relationship with God and knew in my heart that Elk City was the answer. When I discussed the move with others, it was a consensus that it would never work. Elk City had been a rivalry of sorts for years and bad feelings and relationships had been created.

The decision to go to Elk was firm in my heart, and I was certain that the Holy Spirit had confirmed the move. The transition to Elk City was smooth and success was immediate. We became Regional Champions and made our way to the second World Series in program history.

I began to operate in what the Word of God had taught me. Make yourself of no reputation. Give God the glory! He was the focus of our success. I began to give the players and assistant coaches' praise for their hard work. My spirit was in check. I CHOSE to not want the glory. The success was wrapped up in not wanting praise or credit for the success. I had "laid my Isaac down," similar to Abraham laying down Isaac because he had become more important than God. Baseball was that Isaac in my life. It wasn't about pride anymore. We were helping kids gain a perspective that would help them in life.

That foundation transformed into success on the field as well. I learned if you do it the way God planned it, then all things worked out according to His will. He was supernaturally transforming our team concept into an unstoppable organization. The foundation of the Word of God works in every aspect.

This revelation hit home with me in 2008 when I received a call to be the head coach at Elk City High School. I was honored with the opportunity and coaching the high school there was a goal of mine. A local reporter called to interview me about the high school job. He had been covering my summer teams for more than seven years. During this interview, I received an amazing revelation. The reporter began to ask me questions, and I told him about my past baseball success as a player and coach. He was amazed. He had been writing stories about our team for the past seven years and didn't know anything about me as a person, former player, or coach. I answered his questions without feeling prideful. I simply told him the truth.

I told him about my college baseball success at Texas Tech and OU. I mentioned about the High School State Tournament appearances and coaching at OU as well.

It became clear to him and me that not one time over a seven-year period had I mentioned the past or tried to make myself the centerpiece of our program. When we gain this perspective and make God the centerpiece of every conversation, it eliminates the pride. God can move when we give HIM His rightful place at the TOP of our priority list. I had followed His plan and it worked.

We must understand that His foundation is much better than any plan we can dream up. His plan leads to ultimate success, on and off the field. When He is given His rightful place and trusts the person enough to anoint him with the authority to operate, success is inevitable. All who are involved in the process will be blessed and the outcomes will be perfect.

During this seven-year period, the success was at the top of summer select programs anywhere. It wasn't the money or the talent. Those were simply factors that helped fulfill God's work. It was His plan. It is my prayer that coaches can grasp the revelations from this writing. People and players came from all over, and our small Western Oklahoma program was blessed.

This period of time was a work that shows completion. The number "seven" represents complete. Traveler's baseball departed from Elk City in 2009. I prayed that the truth of the success for that time frame be the focal point of what actually had transpired. What was really important had taken place in the lives of those young men. The plan was perfect, the success was great, young lives were changed, and God received the glory!

Photo by CoachesAid Staff

CHAPTER 16
THE NEEDS OF THE MANY
OUTWEIGH THE NEEDS OF THE FEW

When coaching a team, you have to learn to build a philosophy and a foundation to stand on when making crucial decisions, especially during crunch time. Changing our philosophy each time we make a tough decision is basically guessing whether your outcomes will be successful or not. I was tired of guessing and began to look for a way to not guess anymore.

If you can learn enough about your players and teach them a philosophy to build upon, you can begin to make decisions based on "your" foundation and eliminate guessing. It is basically playing the percentages based on the strengths of your group and the understanding that you bring into competition together. It gives stability and security to your decisions.

The best philosophy that I learned is based on team vs. individual perspective. I needed to have a philosophy to determine when it was beneficial to play my bench players or take chances with less talented individuals in a systematic way.

The statement I used whenever deciding to take chances was based on the needs of the "many" vs. the needs of the "few" or the "one."

In a team concept, I began to ask this question each time I made this type of decision.

A team must trust the fact that the coach has their best interests in mind first. Therefore, when we make out the lineup, we play to "win" first. The "TEAM" victory is the highest priority. Therefore, put your best team on the field. Secure the needs of the "many" or group first. Gain trust in your players that you have based the decision on them as a whole and not on an individual.

Once the team is in a position to win or achieve the goal of the group, then the needs of the few or one become the priority. An example would be, if you have a ten-run lead and the game is secure, then you can take chances on an individual basis. A lot of times players and parents believe that their son or daughter is just as good as some other players. That is not their decision to make.

When bench players get their chance and the authority is given to them to have opportunity, it is up to them to perform and create a level of confidence with the "TEAM" to bring a level of group trust to make their way into the crucial points of play. Everyone in the group will begin to understand that the moves you make as a coach are solid and based on a foundation that all can trust. Bench players must take on the responsibility to trust the decisions of the coach and buy into the philosophy of the coach. It is about trust. When a group is on the same page, then victory for the team and individuals can be achieved.

It is about creating an environment that works on all fronts. Being consistent in your moves and philosophy will generate trust and ultimately the highest level of performance. CONSISTENCY is crucial when creating individual and team trust.

When a young player eventually moves into a position to be in the thick of battle, he will remember the philosophy and the opportunity that he has and trust the coach to give him the time to produce the way that he had seen done in the past with other players. That player must understand that he needs to perform, but also that he has earned an opportunity once he has been given the starting nod.

It is about balance. We must create consistency and balance in our decisions with the group. Basically, we are gaining trust.

Have faith in your players. Hold true to the consistency of your coaching philosophy. Teach players about the "truth" of who they are as players, about sacrifice, and commitment. Teach them to Love each other and make the TEAM and others more important than themselves.

Basically, bring them to the understanding that sometimes the needs of the many outweigh the needs of the few. And sometimes the needs of the few outweigh the needs of the many. Once they have been taught the difference and the questions about their playing time comes, simply remind them which philosophy we are using during that point in time. It sounds simple and it is for the most part. Tell them the "truth."

This coaching philosophy is nothing new to the world. The philosophy basically came from God's plan for us. The Lord knew that the needs of the many were greater than the needs of the one. That is part of the reason why He sent His Son. He sent Him as a Substitute for us all. The one was sacrificed as a Savior for the world. Wow! It brings perspective to the coaching philosophy. The VICTORY for "many" was God's focus, He knew the need, and He sent the ONE!

Photo by CoachesAid Staff

CHAPTER 17
THE TIMING OF GOD

If we coach with our priorities in the proper place, I believe God always has a perfect plan.

In 2003 I took the baseball job at a 5A school. It was an opportunity to coach a great group of young men. They were hungry to learn, and God had given me authority over the program to minister to this group.

God had fought my battle to get me this job. We honored Him every step of the way, praying for our players daily and leading them with spiritual truth throughout the course of two years. At the end of the second season, I began to ask God, "What more did He have for us in this job?" I have learned to always feel that some spiritual significance or breakthrough moment for God is on the way. It was!

We were scheduled to play a tournament at Bishop Mc-

Guiness High School. The day was Saturday, March 17, St. Patrick's Day. I thought it was amazing that "Bishop McGuiness" was playing "St. Mary's" on "St. Patrick's Day."

Tragedy took place during this game. A longtime coaching legend had a massive heart attack in the third base coaching box. My team was in the stands waiting to play the next game. Everyone at the stadium was shocked at what had taken place. I had my players go to the bus so we could talk. On the bus we prayed together as a team. We prayed for the coach's family.

Afterwards I started the bus and we began the long trek back to our home. It was long because dead silence was on that bus. You could have heard a pin drop for the 45-minute ride. During this time, the Holy Spirit rose up inside my heart. I knew that this group of boys needed a word from God. I was somewhat nervous for what the Spirit was asking me to do.

We pulled into the field my heart began to beat fast as I stood to address the team on the bus. The message was clear. Eternal life was available for each of them. I explained about this coach who had died. He was a Christian. He had accepted the Lord as his Savior and was in eternity with Him.

At this point, I explained to the players how Jesus Christ is the answer to eternal life, and I led my players in the prayer of salvation.

Their response was amazing, and there was not a dry eye on the bus. The players walked by me one at a time and gave me a hug. An amazing thing had taken place. The "VICTORY" for many players had taken place that night.

Moving to the parking lot, God gave me an opportunity to witness to several players over the next hour. Several players opened up and shared personal testimonies, and there was a breaking of many personal issues that players had carried with them.

When I returned to the bus, my assistant coach remained in the seat with tears in his eyes. He had a God moment. A life-changing moment. He told me that he didn't know of any coach who would have the courage to do what I had done. I told him that the covenant I had with the Lord wouldn't have allowed it any other way.

The Lord had placed me in authority of this team for a reason. There was a destiny in it. Jesus had put Himself out there for me and blessed me.

We have to be obedient enough to facilitate the plan that God knew would take place. I am so thankful for the covenant that we have with the Lord. It is powerful to patiently watch Him do His work.

The conclusion to this story was clear to me. God sent me to this community for two years to build relationships. He placed me in authority of a group that was built on God's trust. He placed me there to fulfill a plan. I had been placed in this situation for two years for one special night and a 15-minute talk on a bus. What we must do is be obedient and willing to put ourselves out there for Jesus. Our Lord will do the rest.

It brought clarity to me of how big and perfect God's plan is. He had set the stage for two years to do a complete work!

Lord, help us to patiently seek Your plan in all things. We are thankful that there is something spiritual that can happen inside of the daily walk. You are constantly building breakthrough for people's lives. We need to be obedient to recognize Your Spirit and step out at the right time. Give us more patience to know when the time is right! Amen.

Photo by CoachesAid Staff

CHAPTER 18
BEING PREPARED

I had a dream that I was playing baseball on a town team league with older men. We were gathered together for fun to play the game. In this dream I was well versed in the game rules and understood baseball at a high level. The confidence I had in my ability allowed me to steal bases and basically do anything I wanted. The experience I had gained from college and coaching at multiple levels had made my reactions sharp, and I was able to help the others with the rules and execution.

Some of the people playing were women and young boys who had very little if any experience with the game. They were unsure of the simple truths about the game, such as how many strikes and balls you could have as a batter. Others didn't even know that you could steal a base. The knowledge of the game varied among the players.

I was enjoying the knowledge and experience that had given me an advantage during the game. I always like helping others, and I made a point to educate others as we played.

The revelation that I gained from this dream began when I hit a single into right field. I rounded first base and it was time for my son Parker to come in and "run" for me. I remember having to leave him at first base to make decisions on his own. He was only nine years old, and most of the players on the opposing team were three times his age and more experienced.

As I walked towards the bench, I looked back at him and saw the excitement on his face. I also felt his insecurity of not knowing exactly what to do. He was very sure of himself in some ways and that pride I knew could be his downfall. The other team had some very crafty players. I knew they could run trick plays on him and deceive him into getting tagged out.

I asked myself the questions, "Did I teach him enough to make it around the bases to home on his own? Would he make a mistake by being deceived and be called out on a trick play on his way around the bases?" I wanted to help him, but he was on his own. I could only stand by from the bench and shout out instructions to him. I was forced to "hope" that he could hear me because there were a lot of voices hollering at him. They were telling him to get a bigger lead and making fake attempts to trick him off the base.

At one point Parker was on second base, which is the furthest place from me and therefore the hardest for him to hear my voice. He had his back turned to the field as the pitcher fake threw to second. The ball was still in the pitcher's hand as Parker looked to the outfield. He was being tricked into running to third. I hollered out for him to stay on the base. At that point, behind the outfield wall in the distance an explosion took place. It was like a volcanic eruption where the smoke and gas were blasting out of the ground.

The game stopped immediately and Parker turned to run to me. The explosion began to move closer and closer to the field. People were scrambling to find safety. The feeling I had was that there was no place to hide. Nowhere was safe!

The world was going up in a cloud of smoke and only those who knew the Lord had security. All were going to perish in the flesh.

God revealed to me that the game is like life. We needed to know the truth from the Word of God to be able to know the game of life and fight the battles of the world. When the players were trying to trick me, it was difficult for them. The players who were not equipped in the rules did not have near the chance of succeeding.

My son Parker needed to grow to a place of knowledge in the game of baseball to make great choices. He needed to be highly educated in the game to succeed on the field. The same holds true in life. If we know the "truth" of the Word, we can be successful in this life. We will be able to avoid the tricks of the enemy. There are many voices crying out to deceive us. We need to know our Father's voice and respond to His truth – the only truth we can trust. I also felt responsible to help others gain knowledge of the "truth" so they could succeed as well. You never want anyone to perish or fail because of lack of knowledge.

The revelation I gained when Parker came in to run the bases for me was, "Is he ready?" He was starting to learn the game and he would have to go through playing it to be able to know it well enough to be great at it. I had to turn loose and hope he could make it around the bases on his own. If he ran the bases enough times, he would eventually gain the knowledge to be his best. He could listen to my instruction during the game when he could hear me.

The next thing I learned is that the game parallels life. My son needed to know the truth of God's Word to not perish. The storms of life will overrun us. We are destined to perish on this earth in the flesh at some point. When the end comes for any of us, will we have security to know that we have eternal life with Jesus?

As I watched my son Parker run the bases, I wanted to help him in the worst way. My heart was totally with him. I wanted to take his place. I asked, "Can I go back in and run for him?" I knew I couldn't. This brought me the amazing revelation: God knew from the beginning that we would make mistakes and fail at times. When He looked out at us being deceived and tricked into getting out the same as I saw my son being picked off the bases, it was obvious that we didn't have enough knowledge of the "Word" to keep from making mistakes.

God sent His Son Jesus back in to run the bases for us. He came in and took all the tricks and deception of the enemy upon Himself. He loved us even more than when I looked at my son Parker and wanted to take his place. It brought me a deeper understanding of why God sent His Son back for us. I would have gladly taken my son's place in this dream. God did that for us. He sent Jesus to take our place. All we have to do is be submitted to His will and the Word of God and allow ourselves to go to the safe place and let Jesus run the race for us. The problem is that our pride keeps telling us we can do it on our own. If we trust the Lord, we CAN hear His voice through the Holy Spirit. He can guide us into all "truth" and hold us back from the deception of the enemy.

Thank You, Lord, for loving us even when we make mistakes!

CHAPTER 19
FROM FAILURE TO VICTORY

As the author of the book, *The Perfect Game*, it was my goal to send the message that at times we all fail. I have failed many times, sometimes miserably. By coaching the sport of baseball, I have been able to look at the substance of this game and what makes it special. "Special" is often a hard word to define. I believe the word "special," when it comes to the sport of baseball, refers to the difficulties of the sport.

The amount of failure that a player deals with in the game surpasses any sport, in my opinion. Often, you hear coaches make the statement, "You can be successful 30 percent of the time and make it to the Baseball Hall of Fame." That 30 percent they are referring to is going three for ten at the plate or at bat. The player who has a career .300 average often makes it to the Hall.

Players are challenged at every level of baseball to handle their emotions and continue to push for excellence in a sport that they are failing in 70 percent of the time. The character that young men and now women face with softball is very valuable in how we are able to proceed in life. I mention many times throughout this book that I have found the most valuable things at the bottom of failure. That is when the metal meets the road – the place where we are forced to make a decision. When life brings us to this place of breakdown, we must choose to continue to fight the fight. Eventually, it becomes joyful to stand in the face of adversity and achieve victory. This is what the Word of God teaches us. Jesus faced certain death at the cross and continued to push forward through the struggle and the pain to achieve the ultimate victory.

As individuals, we are challenged to be victorious. Life and sports prove to us over time that real victory can only be understood when the risk and the consequences of failure are highest. Therefore, we must proceed, knowing that we are to consider it all joy when we fall into certain trials, as it says in the Word. Through the trial, we can find the depth and quality of victory.

It has often been my goal for players on my teams to struggle and break. When they break down, they become moldable and humble. When they get back on their feet, they are changed. I have had several players make it far into college and professional baseball. The foundation that it took for them to get to that place was found at the bottom of the breakdown. At the time, it is often to challenge them and watch them fail, to even push them to the bench and watch them struggle.

I have found myself having to stand in the gap against

players' parents who do not want to watch their sons fail. Oftentimes, these sons choose to quit and blame other factors for their failure. Even more often it is the parent who makes the player quit, sometimes right before the breakdown that was necessary for breakthrough. The bailout of quitting due to this reason only sets individuals back from really growing in character. Breakthrough in character is ultimately what we as coaches should be trying to achieve. When a player gets back up and achieves victory over the sport, he takes with him the value that it takes to become a man.

In God's Word, it says that all fall short of the glory of God. We have failed since the beginning of time. The first failure came in the garden with Adam and Eve. Jesus showed us how to achieve victory in the face of failure. We can fail and rely on His grace to move forward. That is the place where we find ourselves.

In my mind, the game of baseball is the perfect game. Failure is inevitable in this sport. The situations players face throughout a season will force them to make a decision of what they will do with that failure. The choice is ours as coaches to educate them with the truth and the foundation, both found in the Word of God. When we place that solid foundation in front of players expecting the failure to happen, they have the opportunity to fill their lives with the response that will determine their future, on and off the field. The responsibility that players eventually grasp is their own, not that of the coach or the parent. A player can be changed forever with the foundation developed in sports. Baseball leads the way.

The game of baseball has always been unique. We have viewed it in this country as GREAT! I believe this view of the sport comes from down deep in the heart of people, the place where they failed and pushed through, the place that victory and overcoming failure change us forever!

Photo by CoachesAid Staff

CHAPTER 20
THE FOUNDATION FOR SUCCESS

Each time we take on a new responsibility in life, whether it is coaching or in the workplace, we press to know "truth" in every situation.

Truth from the Word that reveals itself to me and that is most certain is that we all fall short of being complete. By "complete," I mean we have to improve at our skills and basic knowledge continuously.

This is mostly revealed to me as a coach, when players are unable to do things and are being instructed to do better.

As coaches we learn that great fundamentals and the best teaching produce the greatest results. Players may not be perfect, but they can be taught from a perfect foundation and a perfect approach, which can only be found in the Word of God. It represents the absolute truth.

Coaching players gives us a look into life and reveals to us what life's obstacles are and how to overcome them. The conclusion I have drawn is that players are not perfect. They need to be taught.

In being taught, they need to gain a "true perspective" as a foundation to receive instruction. This foundation is the same example that Christ gives us in the Bible.

The Bible teaches us that we fall short of perfection and we needed a sacrifice to give us the foundation upon which to build our future. The Word of God says that as we grow as Christians, we will conform to the image of Jesus Christ through the Holy Spirit.

The Holy Spirit revealed to me while I was sleeping that I had found myself taking my players' places. What I mean is that my perspective as a coach became, "It is NOT my players' fault when they fall short. It is mine." When they cannot receive the instruction and fall short of success on the field, I find myself unwilling to place blame on them. I place it on myself.

The enemy assigns blame and accuses. Once players have been taught a task from a great fundamental foundation, they have all the skills and knowledge available to succeed. Sometimes they still fail. When this happens, there should be no blame! The accuser or the enemy is the one telling the player the lies that they carry with them as they fall short. This is why some teams are miserable. The parents, players, and coaches point the finger at each other, dividing the cause and goals and ultimately separating the group from potential success.

This is what happens on a larger perspective in the world. People need to be getting their foundation from the Word of God. As a coach, we must believe in bringing every problem, care, and concern to the light. Players need to be operating in the truth about who they are and that their purpose lays within the team. When they discover this and then place it in the right perspective, they can achieve great things individually and together with their team.

A great truth is found in John, chapter 15, verse 13, KJV, where it says, "Greater love hath no man than this, that a man lay down his life for his friends." As coaches we must find ourselves telling our players that it is our fault. We have obtained knowledge about the game that is above most. The better the fundamentals that we can give them, the faster and further they can develop. They also can develop correctly. The true fundamentals never fail. However, people do.

I received this revelation while coaching. It came to me while I was having my parents' meeting, and I told the Core Group that it was my fault when the players fail. Blame me! I tell the players the same thing. I find myself being willing to carry this burden alone. This is my cross. Parents and players respond to a person willing to lay down himself for his friends. Christ did the same thing for us.

When we operate in the truth in life, we will come to the same conclusion in everything we do, whether it be coaching, teaching, or performing in the workplace or in the home: "We can't do it." Jesus Christ can and did. That is the truth. When Christ went to the cross and the world fell short of acknowledging who He was, He said, *"Father, forgive them; for they know not what they do"*
(Luke 23:34 KJV).

We have to coach a team from the right foundation. This

foundation was created from our existence. It reveals to us that everything we are involved with will bring us back to this basic truth. We needed a Substitute for our sin, our failures, and our shortcomings. Why should it be any different in coaching? We must carry the cross for our players. God put us in a place of authority over a team and the organization. We can place the burden of success on us and then help bring all their burdens to the light and expose the enemy. Take it to the cross and we can be free as a group to do all things.

The enemy can still try to lie and tell us that we failed. He can claim that "we didn't win the trophy." The trophy is only there as the world's prize. It represents an ultimatum that the enemy can make people out to be failures who don't win. Then everyone in an organization has a platform to assign blame to whomever they want.

What we really achieve through sports is a foundation for life. You see, God gave us the perfect foundation with His Word, the perfect fundamentals, and the perfect plan. We fell short, and He took our place. Why should any part of life be any different?

Love should be the foundation, because it took love so deep that God sent His only Son to take our place. Love is the foundation that brings us to success. Love never fails!

Chapter 21
Winning and
the Search for Truth

After being blessed to coach thousands of games and humbly winning many championships, I have discovered that sports provide a very unique look into the spiritual realm. The ability to achieve goals based on hard work and rules in a short-term setting allows us to view a goal and plan and the completion of a plan in a short time frame. We therefore can evaluate the individual behavior as well as the social behavior of a group. The same plan could be evaluated for a bigger group or "life" in general.

In life, whether we know it or not, we are seeking for the "truth." As we grow with the Word of God, the truth in every situation reveals itself to us. The times I have won championships and viewed others winning championships, I have learned one common denominator: An overwhelming "love" comes over the "victory" group. Every other selfish emotion and fleshly plan or desire disappears for a short time and all involved "rest" together through love.

I began to analyze this pattern. What it tells us is that we are searching for something – something that is bigger than winning a game. We are searching for the "truth."

Every team that has fought a tough battle and won a great victory has players that must come to the conclusion that everyone else on the team is more important than they are. Reaching this goal must "outweigh" everything else.

I have seen many players sacrifice everything and humble themselves to achieve a team victory. This act of humility for others is "selfless." When Christ went to the cross for us, He became the ultimate Sacrifice, a complete selfless act to give it all for us. What happened after that is a complete understanding of one word – LOVE. This type of love is repeated on the field of play at almost every hard-fought sporting championship across America each year.

As I began to analyze it even deeper, I have come to another conclusion: To share in this type of love after a victory, the players must be yoked or united by something larger than them. Emotions alone cannot create this overwhelming, unified experience of love. Only spiritual connection between the team can create it.

We as Christians realize that the works of the flesh are adultery, fornication, uncleanness, lewdness, idolatry, sorcery, hatred, contentions, jealousies, outbursts of wrath, selfish ambitions, dissensions, heresies, envy, murders, drunkenness, and revelries.

The fruit of the Holy Spirit include love, joy, peace, longsuffering, kindness, goodness, faithfulness, gentleness, and self-control.

If a team is motivated by the works of the flesh, they could not reach this "love" experience. If emotion alone was the source, then the result for each individual would be different and scattered. Therefore, the common ground love experience is yoked by our desire to search and reach the truth – the truth that God is love and Christ gave us the example of it at the cross. Our inward spirit man desires to be more like Christ. We are able to embrace a part of how God intended our world to be through a championship by sacrifice. Without sacrifice we fail at everything. Each thing we achieve takes one key element – sacrifice.

I tell you the truth through the Word of God. We desire to find ourselves better than what we have here on earth. The deception of the enemy clouds our thinking that "we" are what's important. When we understand that "everyone else" is most important and our sacrifice is for someone else and something else, we yoke up with the Holy Spirit. Then we find something more special than life itself. We desire God through Jesus Christ our Savior.

We desire to win so badly that we fool ourselves into thinking that a trophy or being able to say we are better than others is why we do it, why we sacrifice, and why we suffer for a goal. We do it for complete acceptance. Everyone realizes that the sin in their lives makes them feel unsatisfied and even insecure. When we win a championship, for a short time, under the given rules, we feel accepted or worthy. The root is love and can be found on a regular basis when we know Christ as our Savior.

For most youth, winning on a team becomes their first and maybe only experience of this kind of love and acceptance. As Christians and as leaders, we need to be in position to explain that winning really is an example of unity and acceptance, through love, by achieving in a selfless manner for others.

Photo by CoachesAid Staff

CHAPTER 22
NO STRIKEOUTS

I had a dream about standing in the batter's box. In this dream I remember being afraid that I might strike out. The reason that I am afraid is that I realize I already have two strikes on me when I am approaching the plate.

Being a part of baseball my entire life, I have looked at the success of hitters with different counts. The highest batting average or chance of success is when the count is three balls and no strikes or three balls and one strike. The lowest chance of success comes when the count is no balls and two strikes. These statistics are true from Little League to the major leagues.

The part of this dream that became a revelation to me is the count that I am batting with. I asked the question, "Why do I always have two strikes on me when I get in the batter's box?" The answer was revealed to me. I had been going through life swinging at bad pitches and making bad decisions when the enemy would tempt me.

I realized at this point that the enemy is like a crafty left hander on the mound. He has been pitching the game for a long time and knows the Word of God. He is able to deceive us with tough pitches, especially when we are unable to realize the difference between good and bad decisions or "pitches."

Whenever he would throw me a curve ball that looked good to my flesh, I would swing at it and miss the pitch and that would be strike one, a decision that would represent what a bad choice might be.

Examples of pitches that the enemy might throw at us:

1. *Go to the bar and drink a lot of alcohol.*
   That will fix your problems.
2. *Go ahead and drive. You're not that drunk.*
3. *Dance with that girl who isn't your girlfriend.*
4. *Go ahead and look up pornography on the internet.*
   It is just pictures and it won't hurt anything.
5. *I will act and do like my peers do. That way I can*
   fit in.
6. *Everybody else does these things, so it is okay.*

When we don't know the "voice of truth" that comes from the Holy Spirit of God, we are only capable of listening to the voice of the enemy. He is the only one talking – the one who is leading us into the lies that put us in a no balls and two strike count. The enemy is the author of lies and deception. The Word tells us that we perish by lack of knowledge.

We must be committed to listening to the truth of God's Word and be obedient to it. When we do, we will recognize which decisions the enemy is throwing at us that are bad pitches at which to swing. These are the pitches that we are unable to hit. They put us in the batter's box zero and two. We will walk through life in fear of the next pitch and carry with us the past bad decisions that we have made to put us in that situation.

When we have knowledge of the truth of God's Word, we stop swinging at the enemy's junk. We start taking all those bad pitches as balls and go through life with a three and zero count. With this three and zero count, we are walking through life unafraid of what the enemy throws at us because we are not swinging. We become effective at making good decisions and wait for the fast pitches down the middle that we can hit out of the park. We have joy and peace and others can learn from us how to get in the box against an enemy that can't strike us out.

The bottom line is that we need to teach the Word of God and help others understand the difference between the enemy's plan and God's plan. When we grow in knowledge of the Word, we start to make better decisions. Once you understand the truth, it will set you free, just as it says in the Word. Once you begin to operate in this freedom, you want more and more. It begins to work in your life and you hunger for the truth. That hunger continues to grow and we desire to have more.

CHAPTER 23
PUT YOUR OFFENSE ON THE FIELD
(A DREAM FROM THE HOLY SPIRIT)

One night I awoke from a dream and realized it was very meaningful. In this dream I was on the field playing quarterback. My team was running plays and the success was absolutely zero. We were unable to gain a yard. In fact, we were losing yards on every down.

We were locked down against our own goal line, and I had called a time out. I looked to the sideline and realized that our playbook was completely noneffective. In fact, it became clear to me that the other team already knew the plays we were running before we called them. It was a completely helpless situation, and it was obvious we needed a completely new plan to have any kind of success against this defense.

As I approached the line of scrimmage from my own one yard line, I realized that it was time to surrender my playbook and my ability. It was about dropping my pride and completely giving my future success in this game over to a better playbook and plan. I gained a revelation about what you can do when you are pinned against your goal line. You can take the snap and you can take a knee. I took the snap and kneeled down for a safety.

As I took the knee in the end zone, I looked to the sideline and someone was fastening his chin strap to come in and play quarterback for me. It was Jesus! I realized now that He would take my place calling the plays for me in life. The enemy would be unable to stop any play that He ran. I looked to the sideline, and the coach calling the plays had a book in his hand. It was the Bible, the playbook of life.

His plans and plays for life are way better than mine. I do not have the ability to win this game against the ruler of our flesh and this world. God knew this when He sent His Son to defeat the enemy once and for all. It is about submitting and admitting that His plan is better. It is about getting to the end of ourselves and humbly letting Him become quarterback and call the plays for us.

Every play we run now is going for six points down the field. The enemy is confused and unable to make any adjustments against our offense. It is about being submitted to God's authority and following the plan that Jesus made for us in the Word.

The enemy is now scared to play against our team. He is afraid to even get off the bus, because he is going to get torched for as many scores as we can put on him.

I believe this is the problem with the Church as a whole. We are just glad to be in control of our own lives and would rather be pinned on our own goal line being noneffective and unable to move against the enemy than admit we can't do it alone. If the Body of Christ would simply humble itself to the Word of God and admit that He is right, we could defeat the enemy every time.

It has become clearly evident to me that the Word of God is the absolute "truth." I want Jesus to be quarterback for me every time. When we stand in this type of faith and hold true to the Word of God, then we become unstoppable!

Photo by CoachesAid Staff

CHAPTER 24
THE ULTIMATE AUTHORITY

I had a dream that I was asked to play baseball on a team in a championship game. I was older and had completed my career. The dream began when I arrived at the baseball field. The expectations that I had about the game I would be playing started to change dramatically.

The coach of the team told me to play first base. I was always a middle infielder and had never played first base before. I knew that I was capable to play the position, because I could catch the ball well and it is not a tough position in my mind. I realized I wasn't playing the game for myself. I was playing it for the players who asked for my help.

My concern continued to grow when I was given the glove that I was supposed to use in the game. It did not fit my hand correctly. In fact, the ball was barely able to fit in the pocket. Regardless of the obstacles that I was facing, the game was starting and I found myself on the field at first base.

The ball was hit to the shortstop and players were scoring from second and third base. The throw to me at first would determine whether or not we would win. If I catch it and touch the base, it would be the third out and we would win. If I was unsuccessful, the two runs would score and we would lose the game!

When I looked to the ground, I could not find the base to step on because it was covered with a white tarp. It was a tarp that covered the area about 20 feet around the base.

When the ball was in the air, it was going to be a "short hop" and a tough ball to catch, even if I had a glove that was adequate to do so. As the ball bounced, it was time for me to catch it and I didn't have time to find the base prior to making the play on the ball. I was able to trap the ball with both hands. At this time, I began to step around hoping to find the base and record the out.

The runner then passed me, and I realized that I had missed the base. The obstacles that I had faced in a game that I once thought I was good at had caused me to fail.

I looked at the umpire for him to make the call. He looked at me and called the runner OUT!

I was amazed at the call. I knew that he had stepped in and made the decision for me. I had failed at something that I was supposed to be very good at. The umpire had the authority to make the call. He chose to call him out so my team would win.

I gained a great revelation from this dream. No matter how good we are at something and how many times we are capable of succeeding under OUR own power, the world has a way of stacking the deck against us! God loves us and if we trust in Him, He has the ability to change our outcome even when we fail.

My confidence that I had always had in myself to play the game and make the out had been changed. The world is capable of using our own pride to set up circumstances to defeat us in the things that we are good at.

It was clear to me that I had a pure heart in my intention to help my team win – not for me, but for the others. I also had relied on doing the very best I could to make the play and leave the judgment of the play to the authority in charge. I had relied on God the same way. Even when I had sinned or fallen short in life, He still chose to make me the winner! In fact, Jesus went to the cross to guarantee us victory even when we don't deserve it.

The umpire made the call in my favor. The crowd screamed and hollered at him that he missed the call. They ridiculed him and threatened him. He became the blame for us winning and my failure was placed on him. I was taken out of the place of ridicule.

The revelation that I gained was that of Jesus! He stepped in for us and made the call. He took the ridicule and the blame for our mistakes and said, "Father, forgive them, for they know not what they do!"

When we are under the grace that Jesus bought back for us at the cross, we put ourselves in a position for Him to cover up our mistakes and make the call for us against the accuser, who is Satan.

I realized that something I was the very best at which was "catching a baseball" could be taken from me in this world. The circumstances can trap us and cause us to stumble. Our pride in ourselves also fuels the fire of the accuser who loves to point the finger at us. That accusing comes from the enemy and not God.

I thank God every day for being able to make the call that favors me even when I have fallen short and failed. He has the "authority." He bought the right for us at the cross! He won the GAME of life for us once and for all. In Him we will always get the victory.

Conclusion: Put your trust in God. Accept Jesus Christ as your Lord and Savior. He has already won the battle and will take our side especially when we don't deserve it. He ALREADY did it!

Photo by CoachesAid Staff

CHAPTER 25
LEAVE A LEGACY

A coach has the ability to influence for a lifetime. We must learn that leaving a negative path of influence will cause damage in youth that will someday have to be dealt with by those individuals. There are consequences in the choices we make.

As coaches it is possible to leave a legacy that is harmful to our players. We are often the most impressionable person in their lives. Some coaching tactics might help us win games and could even help individuals become better players on the field, but this doesn't mean that the foundation they were rooted in has positive direction for their growth mentally and spiritually for their future.

In Proverbs 22:6 KJV it says, *"Train up a child in the way he should go: and when he is old, he will not depart from it."*

When you grow in the Lord, you learn that the truth of God becomes clearer. This truth must be the first blocks laid in any foundation for the outcomes to truly be complete!

It goes back to Matthew 6:33: "But seek first the kingdom of God and His righteousness, and all these things shall be added to you."

If this scripture is "true," then we must conclude that seeking God with our team FIRST will cause the result of success on and off the field.

There will be many adverse situations that a team and individuals will face during a season. As coaches our players watch us when we are tested. The way they see our ability to handle adversity and use it to create character for our future challenges is the example that they will hopefully build upon for the decisions they make in the future.

Winning and losing a game cannot be more relevant than the life lesson that is created by each situation. This is the very reason sports was created in the first place. It is a small sample and example of life through which youth learn to handle adversity.

As coaches we have one legacy to truly leave. We cannot guarantee wins, losses, or championships. They are a result of having the most talent and fundamentals. We can control a foundational legacy spiritually that will last a lifetime!

CHAPTER 26
THE TIP OF THE SWORD
(REVELATION OF THE POWER OF THE WORD)

Being a coach and understanding what it means to go to battle to win games, I learned a great revelation.

We are in spiritual warfare. The war is taking place in the heavens, not in the flesh. God is building up a team to fight His battles for Him. The maturity level of Christians varies.

God gave me a revelation whenever I drew the comparisons of sports and going to battle. I had a dream of our team setting on the bench on the sidelines. I was sitting on the bench in the middle, about three players away from the coach. I was anxious to get in the game. I remember knowing that it was a tough battle. Everyone in the game had to be very skilled and capable of fighting at a high level for our team to win. I asked myself what I needed to do for the coach to put me in.

First, I had the desire to be in the game just to make it on the field. Then I realized something great. I wanted to be shortstop and hit third. I wanted to be the quarterback or the point guard. How could I be the "go to guy"?

In this dream, I remember the coach looking down at me and saying, "Check in the game." At this point, he trusted me to fight his battle. This was an awesome revelation. The Coach was God!

SUMMARY

In this dream, it was clear that most Christians make it on the bus to get to the game, but only a few really mature to the point that God will put them in battle. As Christians they are saved, but God won't place them in the battle if they are vulnerable to the enemy. He is a good Father. He will keep us on the bus watching or on the bench until we develop our skills to be in the game. I know God is not a man that He should lie. There are no politics for players to get to play in this game. If He puts you in the game, then He knows you're the choice and ready to make the difference.

As Christians, we have a choice: Be satisfied on the bus or on the bench, not being effective in the Kingdom. Or strive to be the shortstop, the quarterback, or the point guard. When we look at it as the battle that wages on spiritually, it really means we are fighting to the death. We are in a spiritual battle and it's real. People are perishing and the enemy is after souls.

As Christians, we should desire to lead the charge into battle. We are fighting for lives – our family, friends, and people everywhere. When we get the revelation of what is really at stake, we will desire to be the TIP OF THE SWORD!

PRAYER

Lord, I desire to be in the game. Let this revelation bring wisdom and hunger for Christians to not be satisfied with salvation alone. I want to be the TIP OF THE SWORD! Help us all get a revelation of what it means to be in the battle. We may get knocked down or get beat up along the way. You may even need to put us back on the bench to heal up a bit and catch our breath before going back in. I don't want to go to heaven and be one who never was effective in the battle that was taking place on earth!

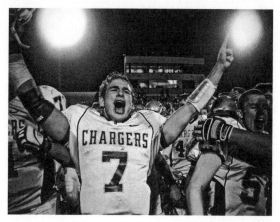

Photo by CoachesAid Staff

CHAPTER 27
VICTORY!

What is victory? It is success in a struggle against difficulties or an obstacle. Victory is the state of having triumphed. Victory refers especially to the FINAL defeat of an enemy or opponent.

Based on the definition of victory, we can conclude that there must be an enemy or opponent before there can be a battle. Therefore, if there is a battle that takes place, then someone will be victorious. If victory also tells us that the defeat is FINAL, then we can conclude that the battle will be finished once and for all!

Team sports allow us to create a situation to battle for victory. It determines the steps and the process we need to follow. We must be prepared for the battle.

In team sports, we will face an enemy on a given date in

time. Our success on the date in time will be determined by who is better equipped. Therefore, we understand that there is a "time frame" that we have to prepare for this battle.

The team that is the most prepared will often be victorious during the battle. To prepare at the highest level for the battle, it takes key foundational character elements. Those elements include: truth, choices, discipline, sacrifice, and love.

When the right foundation is established in team sports, the percent chance of victory increases. One might determine that victory is inevitable.

As coaches we can also conclude that the enemy or opponent is also preparing for this battle. He will do whatever is necessary to be victorious.

The Rule Book and Guidelines are available for any sport that we are playing. Both sides are given equal access to these rules, and it is up to the coaches and teams to use what is at their disposal to prepare accordingly.

If this is true, then we can conclude that knowing the most about our Rules and Guidelines and preparing for "them" will increase our chance of victory. We wouldn't prepare to play a football game and then play basketball!

Coaching teaches us about doing what is necessary to be prepared on game day! That day our skills and knowledge will be put to the test to determine the outcome of the contest. The more times we have been faced with a situation also helps us to prepare in a way to overcome its difficulties and potential changes that are possible, thus leaving us more prepared for the next battle.

If victory in a game is final, then this means that a contest has come to an end! It is final! Then a new time frame is created that we have to prepare for the next battle. Becoming victorious in each contest is a journey! The foundations of character we take with us allow us to mature and grow in our skills and knowledge to be more prepared each time.

In life we face a battle as well. That battle is spiritual and fought for souls. In this battle of life, victory is final. Upon circumstances and death in our flesh, we can be defeated or we can be victorious.

The Rule Book for this game of LIFE is the Word of God. It holds the "truth" for how we can be victorious. Our opponent in this battle is the enemy. He also knows the Word! He knows it very well and will use every tactic to defeat us.

If we are gaining our knowledge on how to live life from the "world," then it comes from Satan's playbook. In the Word of God, it tells us that the enemy comes to steal, kill, and destroy. Those are his tools to bring him victory over us. He doesn't want us to see the Playbook that God created for us. He wants us to be UNPREPARED for the battles we face. Most of the time the enemy is more prepared than we are, perhaps he is all the time. He has had many seasons and battles to learn from. He has a great deal of experience of how to trip us up and keep us from victory.

Jesus came to earth and died for us so that we would have the FINAL victory. We had made mistakes and fallen to the enemy's battle plans too many times. In this game, we were not more prepared than the enemy. We were foolish and chose the wrong things. We had let our sin and fleshly desires rule over us. We were condemned to the destruction that Satan had for us.

Jesus snatched the victory away from Satan at the cross. He bought back our right to be with the Father in Heaven once and for all. The Word of God has the same foundation in it that made Jesus the Victor. It is the foundation that brings us victory as coaches every time. The scoreboard in a game doesn't always say that we were victorious, but the ultimate outcome of a foundation created by God inevitably brings us victory. If facing battles is a "journey," then why shouldn't we coach players with a foundation that will lead them toward the "truth" and eventually the final victory? We must apply this foundation to every aspect of life including our family, children, parents, work, and team. You can't argue with God's plan. We must take the key foundations that GOD Himself gave us and apply them to our teams. God's plan is the only plan that guarantees the true final victory!

EPILOGUE

After an amazing run of receiving God's blessings, I have come to a lot of conclusions. God is love, His Word is the absolute truth, and His plan for each of us is much better than any plan the world can offer.

I have found that the Lord is truly strong when we are weak. In fact, the times when I have found the most joy and contentment are when I have faced obstacles that were too big for me.

Often, I have found myself creating a mountain that was impossible to climb. Therefore, my flesh was forced to give way to the Spirit so God's plan could ultimately be fulfilled.

It is a choice to have the Lord fight our battles. When we humbly allow Him to fight the battles and we apply His Word to our portion of the fight, WE CANNOT BE DEFEATED! He has already won every battle we will ever face!

ABOUT THE AUTHOR

Most people who know me – Mark Ward – call me "Colonel." I never earned such a title, but my dad nicknamed me when I was four years old.

First, I need to get one point across: I have failed miserably at times. I have learned that humility is the place where we come to the end of ourselves, and say, "I can't do it, God." This is when we begin to change.

Sports were the biggest part of my life until Jesus Christ became Lord to me. Growing up in a small town of 200 people in Camargo, Oklahoma, I had very little extracurricular activity to be involved in other than baseball. My father, Bob Ward, coached Travelers baseball, so pretty much every aspect of my life evolved around the sport and the organization.

From being a batboy at age five, later becoming a player, an assistant coach, and then head coach, I was able to get a unique view of how sports relate to life.

My father was blessed to win more than two thousand games during his career, and I have been a part of more than four thousand contests in one way or another. I have lived and died by every pitch and found out what it meant to win and lose.

I learned that sports give a unique view of life. Sports allow us to view behavior in a short-term and small numbers environment. That environment will deliver us success and failure the same way as life. How we choose to deal with it will determine our future success.

The same is true in life. When we face a trial, we must make a choice of how we will react. I have concluded that if we react with the Word of God, and that Word is the foundation of truth, we cannot fail. The same Word will apply to every aspect of life, especially sports. God is that big.

It has been proven in my own life that God cares about every aspect of my life and every decision I make. He cares about my success on and off the field. The Word says that God even knows the number of hairs on our head (see Matthew 10:30). He is God! As you get to know Him more, you will begin to understand that He is that big. He knows all things and He can do all things. The problem we face is the fact that it is our own choice to believe the Word and truly place God first in our lives. That choice determines our future.

Possibly the biggest thing I have learned through sports is, what makes a champion? I had always believed that becoming a champion was based on winning a game or a trophy. That can be the result, but I have learned that in life, everyone gets knocked down and falls down in a variety of ways. I have concluded that a champion is not someone who can rise, but someone who can fall and rise again and again. The fall is not a bad thing. In fact, the most significant things I have learned in life, I learned at the very bottom of failure. This is the place when you hit your knees and cry out to God for help.

This perspective really hit home when I went through a divorce and faced many trials. I remarried three years later, but I was still going through trials. I remember hitting my knees and saying, "God, it can't get any worse." Then it did get worse. I remember it so clearly as I held my wife Carrie. We were both on our knees, crying out to God for help.

In 1998, Carrie and I made a choice. We began to chase God. The Word says, *"But seek ye first the kingdom of God, and his righteousness; and all these things shall be added unto you"* (Matthew 6:33 KJV). If you trust God completely at His Word and are willing to humble yourself to Him and His plan, no matter what, then all these things really mean "ALL THESE THINGS."

When you pour the Word into your heart and humble yourself before Him, everything has spiritual significance. Therefore, the Word and the Holy Spirit will give us a result and a plan based on the truth of the Word.

God created everything, and His Word is absolute. Therefore, everything we see, hear, feel, and dream has significance through Him. We simply must apply His Word and receive the plan and the truth it has for us.

Years of coaching thousands of games with Travelers and watching teams win championships through Coaches Aid has brought out much of the content of this work.

Carrie and I have followed the Lord, and great things have happened for our family. We rededicated our lives through water baptism in 2002. Later that same year, we were baptized in the Holy Spirit. That is when life took on a whole new meaning and purpose. The fire that began to grow in us was based on the Word. Even in our failures, we have been chasing God and the challenges are being turned into His plan. We are moving from glory to glory.

The championships and success of Travelers baseball and the success of Coachesaid.com are only starters for the personal rewards and family victories that we have seen over the past 11 years. The joy of the Lord is our strength. There have been trials along the way, and we have failed often, but God is on the throne. He qualifies and justifies us when we don't deserve it. He restores us when we need restoration. He redeems us when we need redemption. He deserves and gets the glory for it! He is a good Father!

I have been blessed in that God has given me a gift to speak to people and motivate a group. Writing was my weakness, but God continues to equip us if we just ask Him. We must make sacrifices to follow the Lord's plan. It becomes easier and easier to move into the truth found in God's Word. Many times I have shared with people and congregations about God. I believe that God's plan will continue to move forward in my life through this work. He qualifies us and provides the way. After all, it is His plan!

PRAYER OF SALVATION

If you do not know Jesus Christ as your Savior, the Word of God says that today is the day of salvation. Romans 10:13 KJV says, "For whosoever shall call upon the name of the Lord shall be saved."

Pray this simple prayer from your heart and you will be saved, and your name will be eternally written in the Lamb's Book of Life:

Lord Jesus, I ask you to come into my life. Forgive me of all my sins. I repent of my sins before You this day. I denounce Satan and all of his works. I confess Jesus as the Lord of my life. Thank You for saving me! I believe with my heart, and I confess with my mouth that You rose from the dead. I am Saved! Write my name in the Lamb's Book of Life! Today is my God-day with the Lord Jesus! I pray this prayer to the Father in the Name of Jesus! Amen!

If you prayed this prayer with true repentance in your heart,you are saved. You have become a child of God. Jesus tells us in the Word that He will never leave us or forsake us.

CHURCHESAID.COM

Why should you plant your church/ministry online?

To us at Churches Aid, it's a NO BRAINER! But if you need further proof, please read the following:

The #1 question asked on Google is, "WHO IS GOD?" Do you have the answer to that question?

In a monthly view of U.S. Internet activity for top parent companies and web brands, The Nielsen Company found that the average time users spend using Facebook per month grew nearly 10 percent, topping seven hours. Additionally, the number of those actively using the web grew 3.8 percent, to slightly more than 203 million users. If we recognize that there is an average of four Sundays per month that people can attend church and those services average one hour, we can conclude that people are spending almost two church services per week listening to the voice of the world!

Those numbers are derived just from one site and don't

include: Google, Yahoo, and YouTube to name a few! The most shocking statistic is that the average person spends 13 hours per week online (2009 study by Harrison Interactive)! This number compared to the amount of time spent in church of one hour or zero hours per week is staggering to say the least! Churches Aid believes that the online social voice has a foundation derived from peer pressure and from the knowledge of a worldly view – a view that is not coming from the truth found in the Word of God. The Church, as a whole, must position itself in front of the audience that spends thirteen hours a week in front of the computer!

In America, many denominations have declined in worship attendance and membership for decades. Some churches have closed; others have fewer people attending. Over these same decades, however, Internet usage has exploded. Since 1990 the Internet has grown by 100 percent every year. This opens the possibility of using a live video stream to invite new people to worship and enable current attendees who are sick or out of town to worship with their local church. More and more churches are adding video to their recordings. In these days of YouTube, streaming TV and movies, being able to see in addition to hear the service is more affordable and accessible to churches of all sizes. The Internet is a medium for connecting with a new generation of worshippers.

With more than 110 million Americans never or rarely attending church, it's critical that we cross cultural walls and barriers to reach the lost! Don't let the worldwide web be a wall or barrier for you!

Jesus said, "And this gospel of the kingdom will be preached in all the world as a witness to all the nations, and then the end will come" (Matthew 24:14).